The BIG BOOK of tenor sax songs

Note: The keys in this book do not match the other wind instruments.

AVAILABLE FOR:
Flute, Clarinet, Alto Sax, Tenor Sax, Trumpet,
Horn, Trombone, Violin, Viola, and Cello

ISBN 978-1-4234-2666-0

Visit Hal Leonard Online at
www.halleonard.com

Contact Us:
Hal Leonard
7777 West Bluemound Road
Milwaukee, WI 53213
Email: info@halleonard.com

In Europe contact:
Hal Leonard Europe Limited
42 Wigmore Street
Marylebone, London, W1U 2RN
Email: info@halleonardeurope.com

In Australia contact:
Hal Leonard Australia Pty. Ltd.
4 Lentara Court
Cheltenham, Victoria, 3192 Australia
Email: info@halleonard.com.au

CONTENTS

ALL MY LOVING
from A HARD DAY'S NIGHT

TENOR SAX

Words and Music by JOHN LENNON
and PAUL McCARTNEY

ALL THE SMALL THINGS

TENOR SAX

Words and Music by TOM DE LONGE
and MARK HOPPUS

ALLEY CAT

TENOR SAX

By FRANK BJORN

ANOTHER ONE BITES THE DUST

TENOR SAX

Words and Music by
JOHN DEACON

AMERICA

from the Motion Picture THE JAZZ SINGER

TENOR SAX

Words and Music by
NEIL DIAMOND

Moderately

1.

2.

small notes optional

1.
2.

ANY DREAM WILL DO

from JOSEPH AND THE AMAZING TECHNICOLOR® DREAMCOAT

TENOR SAX

Music by ANDREW LLOYD WEBBER
Lyrics by TIM RICE

BE TRUE TO YOUR SCHOOL

TENOR SAX

Words and Music by BRIAN WILSON and MIKE LOVE

Slowly

BAD DAY

TENOR SAX

Words and Music by
DANIEL POWTER

Moderate groove

1.

2.

To Coda

D.S. al Coda
CODA

BARELY BREATHING

TENOR SAX

Words and Music by
DUNCAN SHEIK

1.
2., 3.
To Coda
3
D.S. al Coda
CODA

(It's A) BEAUTIFUL MORNING

TENOR SAX

Words and Music by FELIX CAVALIERE and EDWARD BRIGATI, JR.

Moderately

1.

2.

BEAUTY AND THE BEAST

from Walt Disney's BEAUTY AND THE BEAST

TENOR SAX

Lyrics by HOWARD ASHMAN
Music by ALAN MENKEN

Moderately slow

BEYOND THE SEA

TENOR SAX

Words and Music by CHARLES TRENET,
ALBERT LASRY and JACK LAWRENCE

BLACKBIRD

TENOR SAX

Words and Music by JOHN LENNON
and PAUL McCARTNEY

BLUE SUEDE SHOES

TENOR SAX

Words and Music by
CARL LEE PERKINS

BOOGIE WOOGIE BUGLE BOY

from BUCK PRIVATES

TENOR SAX

Words and Music by DON RAYE
and HUGHIE PRINCE

THE BRADY BUNCH

Theme from the Paramount Television Series THE BRADY BUNCH

TENOR SAX

Words and Music by SHERWOOD SCHWARTZ
and FRANK DEVOL

BUTTERFLY KISSES

TENOR SAX

Words and Music by BOB CARLISLE
and RANDY THOMAS

BREAKING FREE

from the Disney Channel Original Movie HIGH SCHOOL MUSICAL

TENOR SAX

Words and Music by
JAMIE HOUSTON

CABARET

from the Musical CABARET

TENOR SAX

Words by FRED EBB
Music by JOHN KANDER

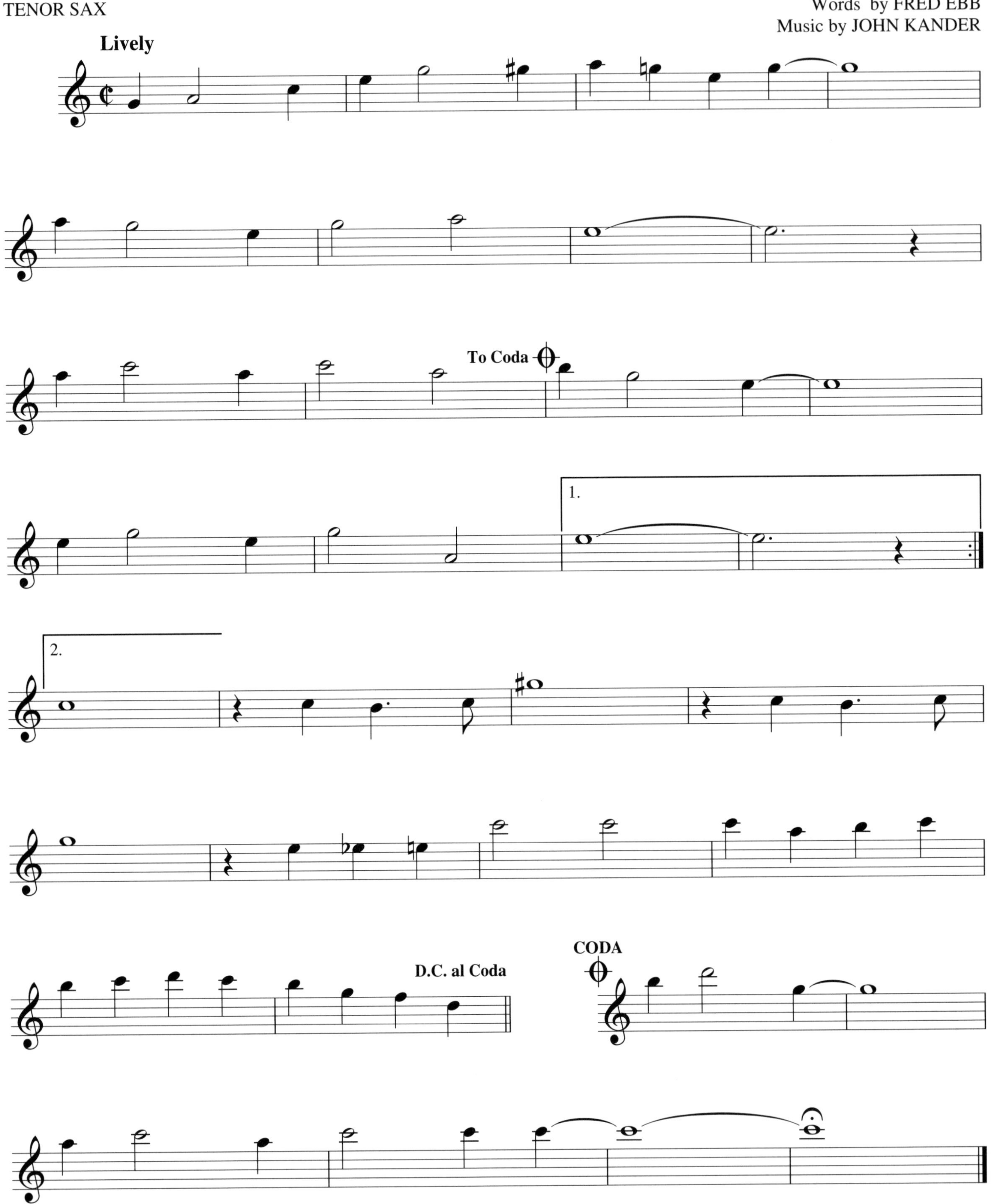

CALIFORNIA DREAMIN'

TENOR SAX

Words and Music by JOHN PHILLIPS
and MICHELLE PHILLIPS

CANDLE IN THE WIND

TENOR SAX

Words and Music by ELTON JOHN
and BERNIE TAUPIN

CHIM CHIM CHER-EE

from Walt Disney's MARY POPPINS

TENOR SAX

Words and Music by RICHARD M. SHERMAN
and ROBERT B. SHERMAN

CLOCKS

TENOR SAX

Words and Music by GUY BERRYMAN, JON BUCKLAND,
WILL CHAMPION and CHRIS MARTIN

Moderately

To Coda

1., 2.

3.

D.S. al Coda

CODA

Repeat and Fade

Optional Ending

(They Long to Be)
CLOSE TO YOU

TENOR SAX

Lyric by HAL DAVID
Music by BURT BACHARACH

Slowly, with a steady beat

COLORS OF THE WIND

from Walt Disney's POCAHONTAS

TENOR SAX

Music by ALAN MENKEN
Lyrics by STEPHEN SCHWARTZ

COME FLY WITH ME

TENOR SAX

Words by SAMMY CAHN
Music by JAMES VAN HEUSEN

COPACABANA
(At the Copa)
from Barry Manilow's COPACABANA

TENOR SAX

Music by BARRY MANILOW
Lyric by BRUCE SUSSMAN and JACK FELDMAN

DO-RE-MI

from THE SOUND OF MUSIC

TENOR SAX

Lyrics by OSCAR HAMMERSTEIN II
Music by RICHARD RODGERS

Lively

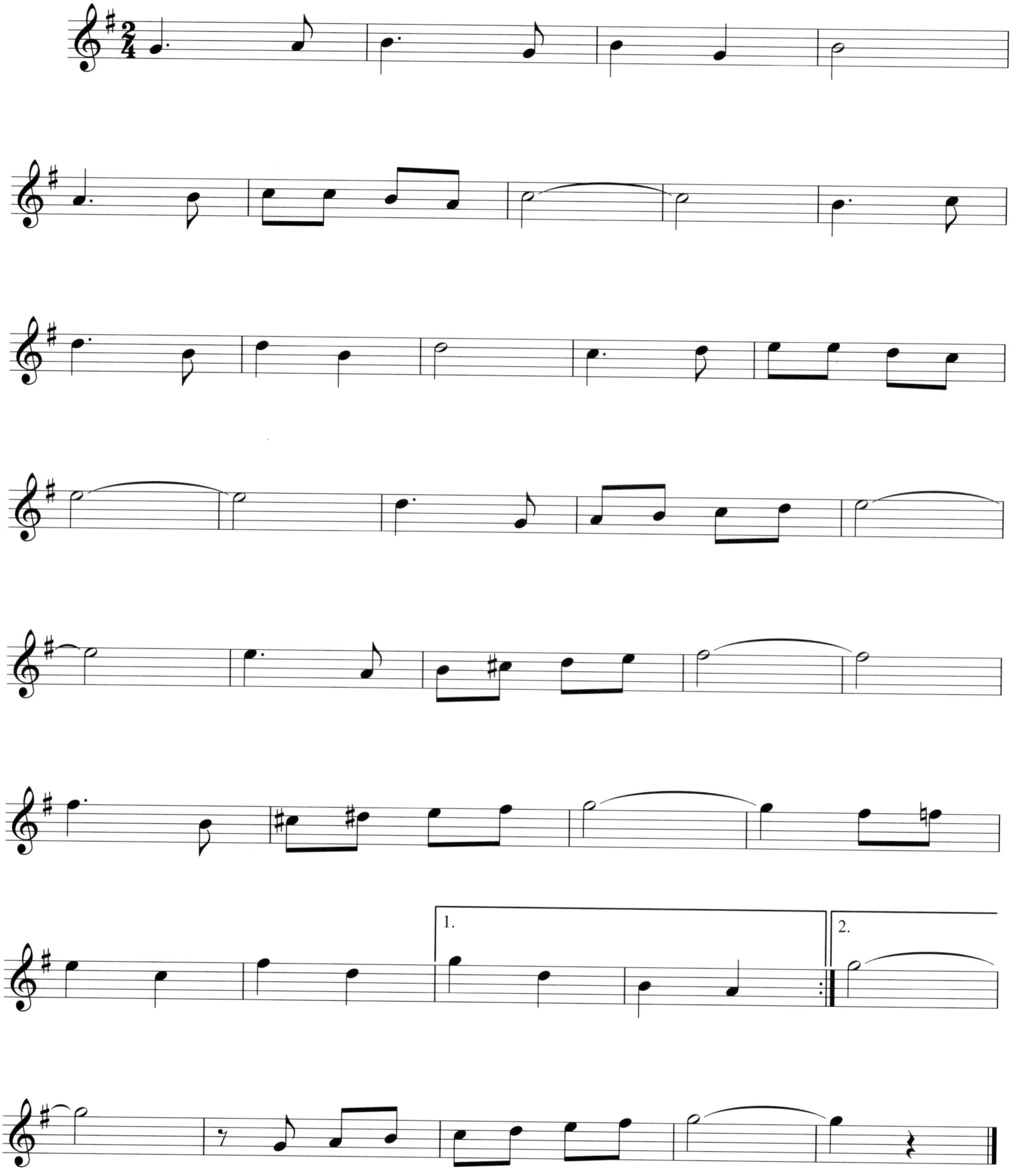

1.

2.

DO WAH DIDDY DIDDY

TENOR SAX

Words and Music by JEFF BARRY
and ELLIE GREENWICH

Moderately

To Coda

1.

2.

3

D.C. al Coda

CODA

(Sittin' On)

THE DOCK OF THE BAY

TENOR SAX

Words and Music by STEVE CROPPER
and OTIS REDDING

Relaxed tempo

1.

2.

To Coda

D.C. al Coda

CODA

DON'T BE CRUEL
(To a Heart That's True)

TENOR SAX

Words and Music by OTIS BLACKWELL
and ELVIS PRESLEY

DON'T LET THE SUN GO DOWN ON ME

TENOR SAX

Words and Music by ELTON JOHN
and BERNIE TAUPIN

Slow Rock

DON'T SPEAK

TENOR SAX

Words and Music by ERIC STEFANI
and GWEN STEFANI

D.S. al Coda
CODA
3
small notes optional

DRIFT AWAY

TENOR SAX

Words and Music by
MENTOR WILLIAMS

DUKE OF EARL

TENOR SAX

Words and Music by EARL EDWARDS, EUGENE DIXON and BERNICE WILLIAMS

THEME FROM E.T. (THE EXTRA-TERRESTRIAL)

from the Universal Picture E.T. (THE EXTRA-TERRESTRIAL)

TENOR SAX

Music by
JOHN WILLIAMS

Energetically

Broadly

Tempo I

EDELWEISS

from THE SOUND OF MUSIC

TENOR SAX

Lyrics by OSCAR HAMMERSTEIN II
Music by RICHARD RODGERS

EVERY BREATH YOU TAKE

TENOR SAX

Music and Lyrics by
STING

EVERYTHING IS BEAUTIFUL

TENOR SAX

Words and Music by
RAY STEVENS

FALLIN'

TENOR SAX

Words and Music by
ALICIA KEYS

1., 2.
3.

FIELDS OF GOLD

TENOR SAX

Music and Lyrics by
STING

FLY LIKE AN EAGLE

TENOR SAX

Words and Music by
STEVE MILLER

FOR ONCE IN MY LIFE

TENOR SAX

Words by RONALD MILLER
Music by ORLANDO MURDEN

Slowly, with feeling

1.

2.

FOREVER YOUNG

TENOR SAX

Words and Music by ROD STEWART,
JIM CREGAN, KEVIN SAVIGAR and BOB DYLAN

FUN, FUN, FUN

TENOR SAX

Words and Music by BRIAN WILSON
and MIKE LOVE

THE GIRL FROM IPANEMA

(Garôta de Ipanema)

TENOR SAX

Music by ANTONIO CARLOS JOBIM
English Words by NORMAN GIMBEL
Original Words by VINICIUS DE MORAES

GOD BLESS THE U.S.A

TENOR SAX

Words and Music by
LEE GREENWOOD

GONNA BUILD A MOUNTAIN

from the Musical Production STOP THE WORLD – I WANT TO GET OFF

TENOR SAX

Words and Music by LESLIE BRICUSSE
and ANTHONY NEWLEY

Moderately bright

1., 2.

3.

GOODBYE YELLOW BRICK ROAD

TENOR SAX

Words and Music by ELTON JOHN
and BERNIE TAUPIN

Moderately slow, in 2

1.

2.

GREEN GREEN GRASS OF HOME

TENOR SAX

Words and Music by
CURLY PUTMAN

HAPPY DAYS

Theme from the Paramount Television Series HAPPY DAYS

TENOR SAX

Words by NORMAN GIMBEL
Music by CHARLES FOX

HAVE I TOLD YOU LATELY

TENOR SAX

Words and Music by
VAN MORRISON

HEART AND SOUL

from the Paramount Short Subject A SONG IS BORN

TENOR SAX

Words by FRANK LOESSER
Music by HOAGY CARMICHAEL

HOGAN'S HEROES MARCH

from the Television Series HOGAN'S HEROES

TENOR SAX

By JERRY FIELDING

HERE WITHOUT YOU

TENOR SAX

Words and Music by MATT ROBERTS,
BRAD ARNOLD, CHRISTOPHER HENDERSON
and ROBERT HARRELL

1.
2.
4

I DREAMED A DREAM

from LES MISÉRABLES

TENOR SAX

Music by CLAUDE-MICHEL SCHÖNBERG
Lyrics by ALAIN BOUBLIL, JEAN-MARC NATEL
and HERBERT KRETZMER

I HEARD IT THROUGH THE GRAPEVINE

TENOR SAX

Words and Music by NORMAN J. WHITFIELD
and BARRETT STRONG

I SAY A LITTLE PRAYER

TENOR SAX

Lyric by HAL DAVID
Music by BURT BACHARACH

Moderately fast

3

I WHISTLE A HAPPY TUNE

from THE KING AND I

TENOR SAX

Lyrics by OSCAR HAMMERSTEIN II
Music by RICHARD RODGERS

I WILL REMEMBER YOU

Theme from THE BROTHERS McMULLEN

TENOR SAX

Words and Music by SARAH McLACHLAN, SEAMUS EGAN and DAVE MERENDA

Moderately slow

I WRITE THE SONGS

TENOR SAX

Words and Music by
BRUCE JOHNSTON

I'M POPEYE THE SAILOR MAN

Theme from the Paramount Cartoon POPEYE THE SAILOR

TENOR SAX

Words and Music by
SAMMY LERNER

IF I EVER LOSE MY FAITH IN YOU

IMAGINE

TENOR SAX

Words and Music by
JOHN LENNON

Medium slow

IT'S MY LIFE

TENOR SAX

Words and Music by JON BON JOVI,
RICHARD SAMBORA and MARTIN SANDBERG

Moderately

1. 2. 2. 1. 2.

IT'S STILL ROCK AND ROLL TO ME

TENOR SAX

Words and Music by
BILLY JOEL

JAILHOUSE ROCK

TENOR SAX

Words and Music by JERRY LEIBER
and MIKE STOLLER

JOY TO THE WORLD

TENOR SAX

Words and Music by
HOYT AXTON

JUMP, JIVE AN' WAIL

TENOR SAX

Words and Music by
LOUIS PRIMA

KANSAS CITY

TENOR SAX

Words and Music by JERRY LEIBER
and MIKE STOLLER

KOKOMO

from the Motion Picture COCKTAIL

TENOR SAX

Words and Music by MIKE LOVE, TERRY MELCHER, JOHN PHILLIPS and SCOTT McKENZIE

LET 'EM IN

TENOR SAX

Words and Music by
PAUL and LINDA McCARTNEY

Moderately

LET'S STAY TOGETHER

TENOR SAX

Words and Music by AL GREEN,
WILLIE MITCHELL and AL JACKSON, JR.

LIKE A ROCK

TENOR SAX

Words and Music by
BOB SEGER

Moderately

To Coda

D.S. al Coda
CODA
3
3
3

LIVIN' LA VIDA LOCA

TENOR SAX

Words and Music by ROBI ROSA
and DESMOND CHILD

Fast, with a steady beat

1. 2.

LOVE AND MARRIAGE

TENOR SAX

Words by SAMMY CAHN
Music by JAMES VAN HEUSEN

LOVE STORY

Theme from the Paramount Picture LOVE STORY

TENOR SAX

Music by FRANCIS LAI

MAGGIE MAY

TENOR SAX

Words and Music by ROD STEWART
and MARTIN QUITTENTON

Moderately bright

1.

2.

MAKING OUR DREAMS COME TRUE

Theme from the Paramount Television Series LAVERNE AND SHIRLEY

TENOR SAX

Words by NORMAN GIMBEL
Music by CHARLES FOX

MAYBE I'M AMAZED

TENOR SAX

Words and Music by
PAUL McCARTNEY

MICHELLE

TENOR SAX

Words and Music by JOHN LENNON
and PAUL McCARTNEY

Moderately

3 3 3

To Coda 1. 2. **D.S. al Coda**

CODA

3

MICKEY MOUSE MARCH

from Walt Disney's THE MICKEY MOUSE CLUB

TENOR SAX

Words and Music by
JIMMIE DODD

MISSION: IMPOSSIBLE THEME

From the Paramount Television Series MISSION: IMPOSSIBLE

TENOR SAX

By LALO SCHIFRIN

MISTER SANDMAN

TENOR SAX

Lyric and Music by
PAT BALLARD

MOON RIVER

from the Paramount Picture BREAKFAST AT TIFFANY'S

TENOR SAX

Words by JOHNNY MERCER
Music by HENRY MANCINI

Slowly

1.

2.

MY HEART WILL GO ON

(Love Theme from 'Titanic')

from the Paramount and Twentieth Century Fox Motion Picture TITANIC

TENOR SAX

Music by JAMES HORNER
Lyric by WILL JENNINGS

Moderately

1.

small notes optional

2.

MY WAY

TENOR SAX

English Words by PAUL ANKA
Original French Words by GILLES THIBAULT
Music by JACQUES REVAUX and CLAUDE FRANCOIS

NA NA HEY HEY KISS HIM GOODBYE

TENOR SAX

Words and Music by ARTHUR FRASHUER DALE,
PAUL ROGER LEKA and GARY CARLA

ON BROADWAY

TENOR SAX

Words and Music by BARRY MANN,
CYNTHIA WEIL, MIKE STOLLER and JERRY LEIBER

Moderately

1.

2.

PEPPERMINT TWIST

TENOR SAX

Words and Music by JOSEPH DiNICOLA and HENRY GLOVER

POCKETFUL OF MIRACLES

TENOR SAX

Words by SAMMY CAHN
Music by JAMES VAN HEUSEN

Moderately, with a lilt

1.

2.

3

PUFF THE MAGIC DRAGON

TENOR SAX

Words and Music by LENNY LIPTON and PETER YARROW

PUT YOUR HAND IN THE HAND

TENOR SAX

Words and Music by
GENE MacLELLAN

QUIET NIGHTS OF QUIET STARS

(Corcovado)

TENOR SAX

English Words by GENE LEES
Original Words and Music by ANTONIO CARLOS JOBIM

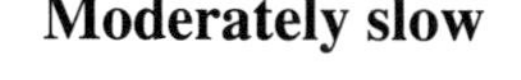

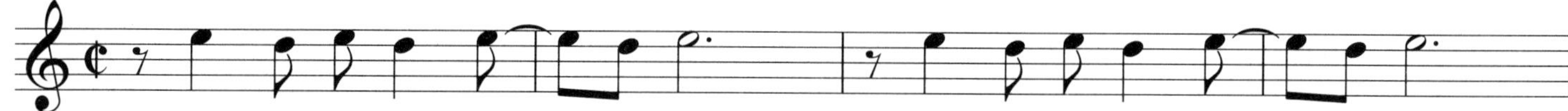

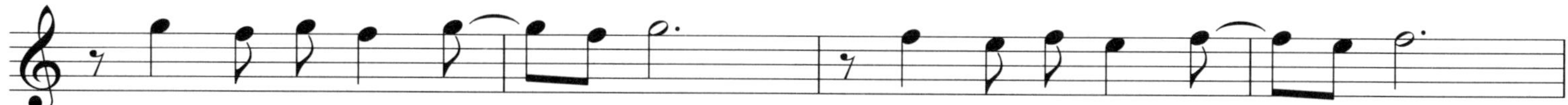

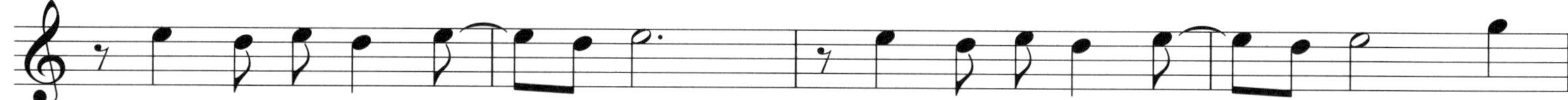

ROCK AROUND THE CLOCK

TENOR SAX

Words and Music by MAX C. FREEDMAN
and JIMMY DeKNIGHT

ROCK WITH YOU

TENOR SAX

Words and Music by
ROD TEMPERTON

SATIN DOLL

TENOR SAX

By DUKE ELLINGTON

SAVE THE BEST FOR LAST

TENOR SAX

Words and Music by PHIL GALDSTON,
JON LIND and WENDY WALDMAN

THEME FROM "SCHINDLER'S LIST"

from the Universal Motion Picture SCHINDLER'S LIST

TENOR SAX

Music by JOHN WILLIAMS

SHE WILL BE LOVED

TENOR SAX

Words and Music by ADAM LEVINE
and JAMES VALENTINE

Moderately

To Coda

1.

2.

D.S. al Coda

CODA

Play 3 times

SING
from SESAME STREET

TENOR SAX

Words and Music by
JOE RAPOSO

SO LONG, FAREWELL

from THE SOUND OF MUSIC

SOMEWHERE OUT THERE

from AN AMERICAN TAIL

TENOR SAX

Music by BARRY MANN and JAMES HORNER
Lyric by CYNTHIA WEIL

SPANISH FLEA

TENOR SAX

Words and Music by
JULIUS WECHTER

STACY'S MOM

TENOR SAX

Words and Music by CHRIS COLLINGWOOD
and ADAM SCHLESINGER

SUNRISE, SUNSET

from the Musical FIDDLER ON THE ROOF

TENOR SAX

Words by SHELDON HARNICK
Music by JERRY BOCK

Moderately slow Waltz tempo

TAKE MY BREATH AWAY
(Love Theme)
from the Paramount Picture TOP GUN

TENOR SAX

Words and Music by GIORGIO MORODER
and TOM WHITLOCK

THAT'S AMORÉ
(That's Love)
from the Paramount Picture THE CADDY

TENOR SAX

Words by JACK BROOKS
Music by HARRY WARREN

THIS LAND IS YOUR LAND

TENOR SAX

Words and Music by
WOODY GUTHRIE

THOSE WERE THE DAYS

TENOR SAX

Words and Music by
GENE RASKIN

TIME AFTER TIME

TENOR SAX

Words and Music by CYNDI LAUPER
and ROB HYMAN

Moderately fast Rock

To Coda

1.

2.

D.S. al Coda

CODA

A THOUSAND MILES

TENOR SAX

Words and Music by
VANESSA CARLTON

2.
D.C. al Coda
CODA

TOMORROW

from the Musical Production ANNIE

TENOR SAX

Lyric by MARTIN CHARNIN
Music by CHARLES STROUSE

TOP OF THE WORLD

TENOR SAX

Words and Music by JOHN BETTIS and RICHARD CARPENTER

TWIST AND SHOUT

TENOR SAX

Words and Music by BERT RUSSELL
and PHIL MEDLEY

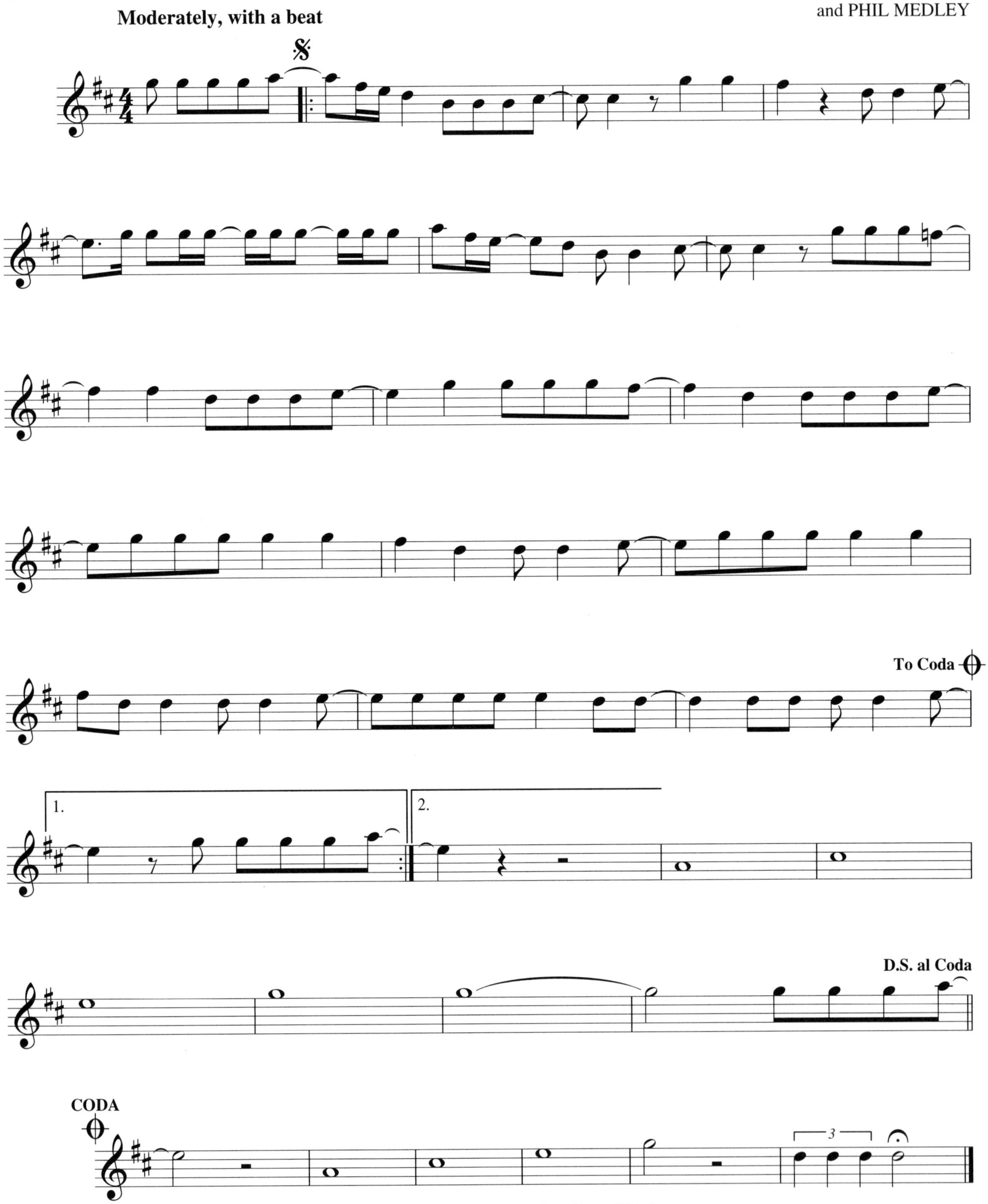

Moderately, with a beat

To Coda

1. 2.

D.S. al Coda

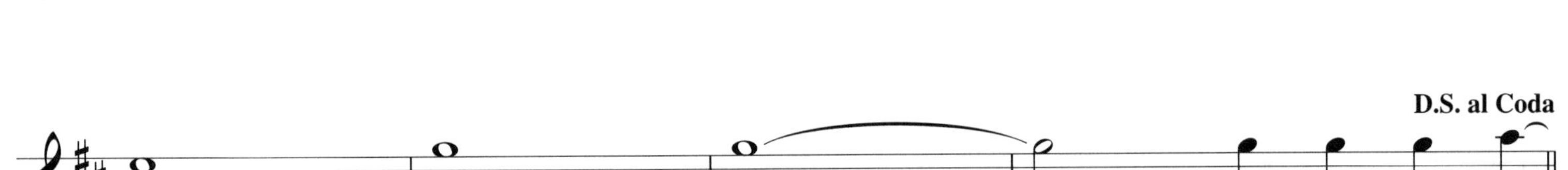

CODA

UNCHAINED MELODY

TENOR SAX

Lyric by HY ZARET
Music by ALEX NORTH

UNDER THE BOARDWALK

TENOR SAX

Words and Music by ARTIE RESNICK
and KENNY YOUNG

Moderately, with a beat

UNITED WE STAND

TENOR SAX

Words and Music by ANTHONY TOBY HILLER
and JOHN GOODISON

Moderately

To Coda

1.

2.

D.S. al Coda

CODA

1.

2.

THE WAY YOU MOVE

TENOR SAX

Words and Music by ANTWAN PATTON, PATRICK BROWN and CARLTON MAHONE

Moderate groove

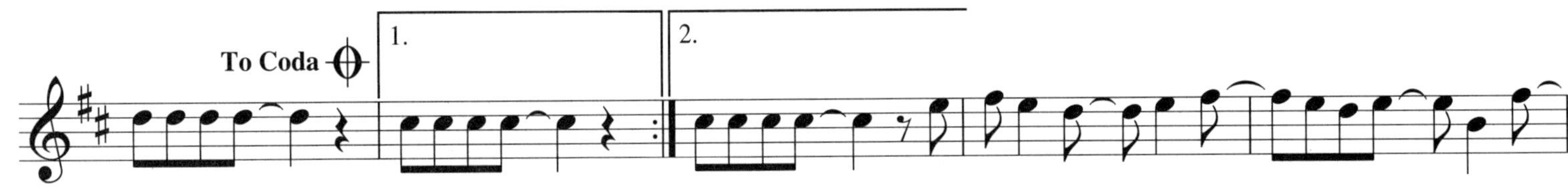

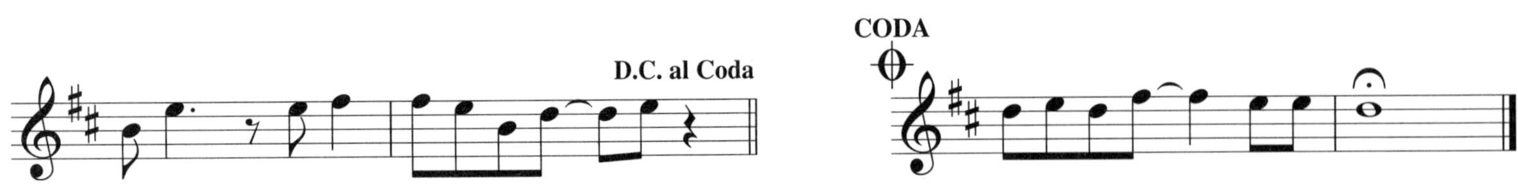

WE ARE THE WORLD

TENOR SAX

Words and Music by LIONEL RICHIE and MICHAEL JACKSON

Moderately slow

3

𝄋

To Coda 𝄌

1.

2.

D.S. al Coda

CODA 𝄌

WE BELONG TOGETHER

TENOR SAX

Words and Music by MARIAH CAREY,
JERMAINE DUPRI, MANUEL SEAL, JOHNTA AUSTIN,
DARNELL BRISTOL, KENNETH EDMONDS, SIDNEY JOHNSON,
PATRICK MOTEN, BOBBY WOMACK and SANDRA SULLY

- contains elements of "Two Occasions" by Darnell Bristol, Kenneth Edmonds and Sidney Johnson and "If You Think You're Lonely Now" by Patrick Moten, Bobby Womack and Sandra Sully

To Coda
D.S. al Coda
CODA

WHAT THE WORLD NEEDS NOW IS LOVE

TENOR SAX

Lyric by HAL DAVID
Music by BURT BACHARACH

WITH A LITTLE HELP FROM MY FRIENDS

TENOR SAX

Words and Music by JOHN LENNON
and PAUL McCARTNEY

WONDERFUL TONIGHT

TENOR SAX

Words and Music by
ERIC CLAPTON

WOOLY BULLY

TENOR SAX

Words and Music by
DOMINGO SAMUDIO

YELLOW SUBMARINE

TENOR SAX

Words and Music by JOHN LENNON
and PAUL McCARTNEY

YOU ARE THE SUNSHINE OF MY LIFE

TENOR SAX

Words and Music by
STEVIE WONDER

YOU RAISE ME UP

TENOR SAX

Words and Music by BRENDAN GRAHAM
and ROLF LOVLAND

YOU'VE GOT A FRIEND

TENOR SAX

Words and Music by
CAROLE KING

ZIP-A-DEE-DOO-DAH

from Walt Disney's SONG OF THE SOUTH
from Disneyland and Walt Disney World's SPLASH MOUNTAIN

TENOR SAX

Words by RAY GILBERT
Music by ALLIE WRUBEL